THE
FOUNDER'S
CHECKLIST

M. L. Bittle

Copyright 2012 by Michael Bittle

All rights reserved. This book, or parts thereof may not be reproduced without permission.

ISBN 978-1-300-22298-9

Contents

Preface..5
I. Overview 7
II. Product..11
   A. Need.. 12
   B. Proprietary Solution....................... 23
   C. Roadmap................................... 37
III. Target Market............................... 47
   A. Market Size................................ 48
   B. Market Dynamics 57
   C. Key Players................................ 65
IV. Company Location 71
   A. Legal Presence 72
   B. Physical Presence......................... 75
   C. Virtual Presence........................... 81

V. Key Personnel 87
- A. Principals 88
- B. Key Technologists 91
- C. Structure 95
- D. Vulnerabilities 101

VI. Funding Sources 107
- A. Key Funding Requirements 108
- B. Best Fit Sources 115
- C. Specific Entities 123

VII. Pro Forma Financials 127
- A. Capital Flows 128
- B. Cash Flows 135
- C. Operational Benchmarks 143
- D. Target Valuations 151

VIII. Exit Strategy 159
- A. Initial Investment 160
- B. Long Term Strategy 163
- C. Contingency Plan 169

IX. Other Stuff 173

About The Author 177

Preface

This notebook is a companion to The Founder's Checklist Template available free at http://www.thefounderschecklist.com The template can be pasted into any text editor to create the working document. Use this notebook as a scratch pad to capture the raw materials that will eventually find their way into that document. Just jot notes here, not fully formed entries (there's not enough room). Besides, you'll want to get those into the template on your computer anyway.

The completed notebook and template form the foundation for your pitch and operational plans going forward. The more detail you can provide for each of the line items in this book, the more likely you will receive funding and achieve eventual success.

I do want to point out that this is not a training guide, or "Startups For Dummies", but rather a memory jogger and data collector. If you're unsure about terms or content, find a mentor, advisor or consultant to assist you. There are a lot complex issues to wrestle here. Any veteran entrepreneur will tell you: now is not the time to figure it all out on your own.

I
Overview

This section is an outline of the topics covered in The Founder's Checklist. They are broken out by sub-topic for note taking from Section II on.

I. Overview

A. Product

What specific product will be the focus of the initial investment?

What is the roadmap?

B. Target Market

What industry (NAISC code) will the product be primarily targeted towards (first release)?

C. Company Location

Where will the company be incorporated, where will key functions reside?

D. Key Personnel

Who are the principals, key technologists? What is the team structure?

E. Target Funding Sources

Which type of funding source best suits company, business model?

F. Pro Forma Financials

Show Capital flows, cash flows projections, operational benchmarks, target valuations/milestones.

G. Exit Strategy

When and how does each investor class realize gains?

H. Other Stuff

Anything that wouldn't fit anywhere else.

II
Product

In this section you capture your thoughts on defining the compelling value of the product.

II. Product (continued)

A. Need

Your new venture seeks to fill an unserved or ill-served need. Use these questions to define your value proposition and demonstrate your domain expertise.

What important problem does the product solve?

How well is the problem understood, how broadly acknowledged by the target market?

What is the current workflow/process flow in the absence of this product?

What are the resultant cost/time implications of that workflow/process?

How significantly does the product address those cost/time implications?

II. Product (continued)

B. Proprietary Solution

You need to clearly identify and position the uniqueness of your solution. Use these questions to help you capture not only the core technology, but also how your competitive position will be protected/maintained going forward.

What exclusive company owned intellectual property solves the problem?

What barriers to entry are overcome or created by this proprietary solution?

What alternatives have been investigated/discarded?

(How will competition likely approach the problem)?

What is the time horizon for competitive advantage?

How extensible is the core proprietary technology/how long can competitive exclusivity be maintained?

What technology shifts could undermine this solution (e.g. hardware costs, materials science discoveries)?

II. Product (continued)

C. Roadmap

There are key transition points as you move from idea to product to company. In this section, the questions are meant to help you articulate the milestones, demonstrate awareness of those transition points and, ideally, your plan for addressing them.

What is the overarching product strategy/vision?

What additional products are envisioned as part of that strategy/vision?

What is the anticipated schedule/frequency of product introductions?

What additional IP is required to implement (developed or acquired)?

III
Target Market

Jot notes here about how you define the marketing objective in the context of the target customer base.

III. Target Market (continued)
A. Market Size

Another aspect of planning beyond a product towards a business is sizing the opportunity. Here is where you capture the characteristics that determine the size of the opportunity. You'll use this to justify the effort and any initial investments.

Describe the total market size (top line sales volume of participants).

Describe the type and number of participants.

What are the total annual expenditures on similar technology/products?

Focus on and describe the total market size for the targeted product.

III. Target Market (continued)

B. Market Dynamics

In order to get a clearer picture of the opportunity, one needs to look beyond static market projections and understand the underlying dynamics. These questions help give you a clearer picture or the business environment you're targeting.

What is the nature of your target market's dynamics? (e.g. seasonal/cyclical/event driven/constant.)

How mature is the target market? (e.g. growth, established, or consolidation.)

To manage your sales funnel, what is the typical approval cycle for similar purchases.

III. Target Market (continued)

C. Key Players

These questions are another facet of demonstrating domain expertise. Knowledge of the competitive landscape and key potential customers will help navigate market uptake.

What are some of the specific companies (customers) that represent "influencers" in the industry?

Who are the specific suppliers of 'competitive' solutions?

IV
Company Location

In today's global economy, there are many implications related to where you do business, on many levels. Record the key details here.

IV. Company Location (continued)
A. Legal Presence

Unless you're selling to friends and family, real companies will want to know your legal business address. (Mostly they want to know you <u>have</u> a legal business address.)

Record the locale of official residency/incorporation.

IV. Company Location (continued)
B. Physical Presence

Aside from where you've registered your business, you may have a different location that is the main office for the company, where the key executives might be based. Also, in this global day and age, some key personnel may operate from other locations. Note that here.

What is your physical Home Office location, and that of any Field Offices.

Record geographic locations of Key Personnel.

IV. Company Location (continued)
C. Virtual Presence

You should call out any vital services/ locations that are not under your direct control, including key staff working from home.

List any current or planned out-sourced services (supply chain and distribution).

List any Key Personnel who will primarily be working from virtual locations.

V
Key
Personnel

How you showcase your team is a key

determining factor in obtaining funding.

Understanding your team is key to scale.

Capture key aspects of your core team here.

V. Key Personnel (continued)
A. Principals

This is as important to the founders as it is investors. Define who does what and understand everyone's backgrounds. Do your due diligence before the investors do.

List all founders including roles brief biographies and sources (e.g. LinkedIn).

V. Key Personnel (continued)
B. Key Technologists

Not all founders are techies, but someone has to actually make something. Here's where you show the depth of your team.

List other key technologists including roles brief biographies and sources (e.g. LinkedIn).

V. Key Personnel (continued)

C. Structure

Roles and responsibilities, who's driving the bus, who are the advisors and fiduciaries. This is the template for scaling the human side of the enterprise.

Describe your corporate governance (e.g. diagram an organization chart including outside directors and advisors).

Describe Project/Product management execution (e.g. who, what, when).

V. Key Personnel (continued)

D. Vulnerabilities

Defining your weaknesses and vulnerabilities before they are discovered in due diligence is good. Having a plan in place to handle them is better.

What aspects of the business rely on a single individual?

What are the contingency plans?

VI
Funding Sources

All your constituents require research and management. Funding is no different. Target these sources as you would your market. Understand their needs and objectives.

VI. Funding Sources (continued)
A. Key Funding Requirements

Treat your funding as a supply chain. Understand your component needs, type of supplier and optimum business arrangement.

What level of investment do you need to advance to the next stage of your venture?

How many investors do you want to manage?

What is your optimum deal structure? (Having a plan B would also be useful.)

VI. Funding Sources (continued)
B. Best Fit Sources

More important than get funding is getting it from the right source, one that's compatible with you, your company, your market. Here are a few ways to cut the deck.

For each investor type (e.g. Angel, VC, Corporate Investment, Banking) rank for best fit.

List any known investors in similar technologies (past and/or present).

List any known investors in target market companies (past and/or present).

VI. Funding Sources (continued)

C. Specific Entities

As you build you list of potential funders, capture all the vital stats here.

Note the key information for possible funding sources (e.g. company names, principals, contacts) here.

VII
Pro Forma Financials

If you can't measure it, you can't manage it and the measurement of business is money. Know and show where it comes from and how its used.

VII. Pro Forma Financials (continued)
A. Capital Flows

Whether you prepare a formal B school business plan or not, you still have to follow the money. Starting with the big bucks.

What are your capital flows for the first year?

What is the anticipated term of the initial investment?

How much capital is the forecast need to reach to break even ($BEP/VBEP)?

VII. Pro Forma Financials (continued)
B. Cash Flows

This is where the rubber meets the road. At the end of the day, how are you planning on paying your bills.

What are your forecast first year cash flows?

Show cash flows over the term of the initial investment.

Show the cash flows forecast to reach break even ($BEP/VBEP).

VII. Pro Forma Financials (continued)
C. Operational Benchmarks

How will you measure how you're doing. These are a few things that investors are going to want to hold you to.

When is your projected first product (revenue) shipment?

When do you forecast positive cash flow from Operations?

When do you forecast break even for the overall business ($BEP, VBEP)?

VII. Pro Forma Financials (continued)
D. Target Valuations

Investors have yield/time objectives. They also have different methods of valuing a business. Having a reasonably defensible estimate for the appropriate valuation type may help you in selecting the type of investors you are seeking as well as possible exit strategies.

What is the median Sales Multiple valuation for your market/business type?

What are your target Capitalization valuations at major milestones?

What are your projected Book Value
valuations at major milestones?

VIII
Exit Strategy

No condition is permanent. Plans change. Life happens. How do you and your investors move on. You should think through your goals and understand those of your investors.

VIII. Exit Strategy (continued)
A. Initial investment.
Understand your initial investors term horizon and return needs.

How and when do initial investors exit?

VIII. Exit Strategy (continued)
B. Long term strategy.

Here's where you define the end game. Also, as you grow, you'll need more capital. Show how you'll handle transitions, early exits, dilution.

What are the follow-on investments?

How do the principals transition?

VIII. Exit Strategy (continued)
C. Contingency plan.

Here's where you flesh out how you'll handle funding discontinuity, shortfalls and timing misalignments.

How will you recover in the case of unanticipated scenarios?

IX
Other
Stuff

Just in case there is something you find important that doesn't have a home in the outline, or if you need more room to ramble on a topic, put it here..

IX. Other Stuff (continued)

If you're using this section to continue notes on a earlier topic where you ran out of space, it's probably a good idea to note the section number so you can trace back later.

About The Author

Michael Bittle is a Technology and Operations Coach, and creator of The Bittle Code(sm) for growing your business. He works with Founders, CEOs and Investors who want to take their entrepreneurial venture and build a scalable company for growth or exit.

Find more information and follow the blog at:
http://www.thebittlecode.com

www.ingramcontent.com/pod-product-compliance
Lightning Source LLC
Chambersburg PA
CBHW060849170526
45158CB00001B/284